Tiggy

The TIGER Cat's Long Journey to Friendship

by Geoff Swift

Design and Illustration ©2023 by Jane Cornwell
www.janecornwell.co.uk

Published 2023 by Jane's Studio Press

ISBN: 978-1-7393231-7-2

Also available as an ebook and in Large Print Size 18 Open Dyslexic Font on cream paper.

To Rona, my wife, for her support and
encouragement to continue writing.

And
Jane Cornwell who has supported and shared my
writing journey, by illustrating all my books. A nice
person with a special talent.

Geoff Swift

Contents

Chapter 1

Tiggy woke up, slowly opening her eyes. Her gold-flecked eyes were just slits as she looked around in the bright sunlight. A strange noise or something else had disturbed her sleep. She slowly arched her back, stretched her legs, then stood up. Motionless, she sniffed the air and then twitched her ears. The noise was coming from next door. What was going on? How dare they disturb her sleep! She decided to find out.

Everyone in the neighbourhood knew Tiggy as Tiger because of her reddish-orange and cream stripes, which made her look like a miniature Tiger although her name was Tiggy. She stretched once more, yawned, then slowly ambled across the

garden stopping every so often to look around.
When she reached the garden fence, she sprang
up landing on a fence post. She sat on the post, her
long striped tail hanging down, slowly swishing from
side to side, as she narrowed her eyes and watched.
The noise was coming from next door. She took one
long look, then made up her mind to find out what
was happening. Jumping from the fence she landed
silently and perfectly balanced on the ground, then
looked around the garden next door. What was
going on? There was a big van on the road outside
the house, and men were carrying furniture and
boxes out of the house. This house was in her
territory, how dare they upset her by changing it,
she thought. She decided to investigate further.

She slowly walked to the back of the house
and noticed the backdoor was open! Casually
peeking inside, she could see the humans packing
boxes, and taking the furniture out to the van.
Tiggy stepped into the kitchen to explore further.
She sat in the middle of the kitchen floor, her tail
stretched out like a question mark, and watched.
Where were the humans she had trained? Why
were these strange people taking everything out of
the house? Tiggy had to find out.

She slowly walked from the kitchen into
the hall. 'GET OUT OF THE WAY CAT!' one of
the strange people shouted at Tiggy. Tiggy only
responded to humans she had trained. Tiggy's hair

FRAGILE
This way
KITCHEN
FRAGILE

bristled, and she arched her back.

'How dare these strangers shout at me, this is my territory,' Tiggy thought crossly.

When the stranger shouted at her, one of the owners of the house came out of the lounge. 'Tiggy!' she exclaimed, 'You're in the way, come on, I've got some cat treats you can have before we go.'

Tiggy didn't understand human talk, but she knew kind words and tones. The lady lifted Tiggy into her arms, scratched under her chin then carried her into the kitchen. She took a box of cat treats from a cupboard. Putting Tiggy down she poured cat treats onto the kitchen floor for Tiggy to eat.

Tiggy looked at the treats, then up at the woman. Something was wrong. Tiggy could sense it. The lady bent down and stroked Tiggy. 'Go on Tiggy eat your treats, it's the last time I'll be able to give you them. We are moving far away, and I'll not see you again.' Tiggy could tell by the tone that something was really wrong. The lady sounded sad. As Tiggy watched, the lady turned and put her hand to her face to wipe away a tear, took a deep breath, then walked away to talk to the strange people in the house. Tiggy watched her walk away then focused on the treats, these were her favourites, so she tucked in.

When she finished her treats, she sat back and watched as the house was emptied. She watched as they carried out her favourite chair. This was enough for Tiggy, there was no way she was being parted from that chair. It was the most comfortable chair to sleep in and it was hers. She ran out of the house and watched as the chair was put into the big van. She waited until everyone was back in the house, then jumped into the van looking for her chair. She found it at the back of the van, she then jumped into the chair, curled into a ball, and went to sleep.

Chapter 2

Tiggy woke up to the gentle swaying of the van, and the drone of the tyres on the road. She quickly sat up and looked around, she was trapped inside. The doors of the van were shut, and they were moving. Tiggy looked around. She WAS trapped! She lay down on her seat to think. The only time she had travelled was in a car, usually in a cage when she was taken to a place with lots of other animals where she would end up on a table. There she would be prodded and felt. Sometimes they would even stick a needle into her. She hated being in a car and this was no better, the difference being it was a big van, and she wasn't in a cage. Realising there was nothing she could do, she settled down to wait.

After several short stops and starts the van finally stopped. Tiggy stretched out to ease her muscles, then jumped down from the chair. She could hear voices outside, so she hid behind a unit at the side of the van. Suddenly the interior of the van was bathed in light as the van doors opened. Tiggy waited and listened. The voices disappeared so Twiggy slowly looked out. There were the strange people walking up a path to a house with their backs to Tiggy. This was her chance to escape from the van. She ran down the van, leapt onto the pavement then ran to a clump of bushes from where she could see further along the pavement. She dived into a bush, sat down, and slowly looked around. She peered out of the bush, it seemed to be safe here, she needed time to think. She was lost, this was all unfamiliar territory.

She sat down and looked through the leaves to the sky. The sun was on her right-hand side, she slowly turned so the sun was on her left-hand side and looked North. Her territory should be in that direction. She looked around again, but there was nothing she recognised. She was lost! Tiggy shivered, she was frightened and didn't know what to do. In her territory, she knew everything and everyone, but she knew no one here, and she wanted to cry. She lay down under the bush, stretched out her legs and put her head on her front paws, then cried herself to sleep.

Tiggy woke up with a start, she lay motionless but rotated her ears and focused. There! Further up the road were two dogs, they were growling at each other, and that's what wakened her up. Tiggy sat up, licked her front paws, and washed. She watched as the dogs walked up the road until they were out of sight. She knew it was no good feeling sorry for herself, she was in trouble it was up to her to do something about it. She needed to find her way home. She crawled out from the bush and then sat on the pavement. She needed a plan. First, she needed to get food and something to drink, then she could start off towards her own territory and her home.

She looked around and sniffed the air. She could smell cooking fat in the air from a fast-food restaurant, normally she would never go near these places as she didn't like the food. However, today she was hungry and knew that there would be scraps of food that had been dropped that she could eat. Tiggy used her nose following the smell of the fast-food restaurant. There were rubbish bins outside which were overflowing with discarded food and discarded wrappers. Tiggy looked around checking it was safe and jumped up onto the bin. The smell was disgusting, normally Tiggy would never have gone near it. However, she needed food. She balanced on top of the bin stretched

out a front paw, unsheathed her claw then fished around in the bin searching for food. She found a half-eaten burger. She hooked it with her claws and fished it out. Putting it in her mouth to hold it she jumped down from the bin. She saw a bench further along on the pavement. She ran to it, then sat underneath to eat the burger. When she finished, she sat back and licked her lips, the burger had been a bit greasy, but it was food. Tiggy then wet her paws washed her face then sat and lay while she cleaned herself. She may be lost but she wasn't going to let herself get dirty. After she had cleaned herself, she took one last look around. 'Right! I need to get away from here and head for home.'

Chapter 3

Tiggy looked up at the sun and decided on the direction of home. She walked through the town and then into the countryside all the time watching the traffic and the people. After four hours of walking, things were quieter, with less traffic, and no people. She was surrounded by fields, and it was getting dark. She needed to find a safe place to sleep. She walked along a drystone wall dividing a field until she found a spot where some large stones had fallen from the wall. The fallen stones created a natural shelter at the base of the wall. Tiggy climbed over the fallen stones and found a sheltered spot where she could curl up and go to sleep. She took one last look around, then up at the stars, lay down and curled up into a ball and quickly fell asleep. She was exhausted after a very long and trying day.

Tiggy woke when she felt something breathing on her. She slowly stretched out her claws ready in case she needed to fight or scratch. She slowly opened her eyes. There, looking down at her, were brown eyes in a big black face with a black shiny nose. It was a sheep.

'Hello' the sheep said. 'What are you doing here? You're not from the farm as I know all the farm animals.'

Tiggy sheathed her claws, stretched, and sat up. 'I'm Tiggy and I'm heading home' she replied.

The sheep looked at her thoughtfully, 'You must be lost, there are only farms around here and I know most of the animals. Do you know where your home is?'

Tiggy nodded her head and said, 'I think it's in that direction.'

The sheep let out a 'Baa' chuckle, 'So you're lost and think your home is that way. Well, there are lots of farms and animals in that direction, let me see if I can help you to get home. If you've been out here all night you must be hungry. Come on, follow me, and I'll get you some food. I've got a clever friend we can rely on; he'll be able to help.'

As the sheep walked off Tiggy shouted, 'Stop! What's your name?'

The sheep stopped and looked back at Tiggy, 'Olivia' she replied 'but my friends call me Oli. You can call me Oli if you want.'

Oli turned and walked away. Tiggy took a quick look around then ran across the field to catch up. Oli told Tiggy she was looking for her friend Tom who was very clever and would be able to get food for Tiggy and help her to get home. As they talked, they passed a flock of sheep who stopped to look at the pair.

'Who's your new friend Oli?' one of the sheep shouted.

'This is Tiggy, and she's lost, I'm looking for Tom to help her. Have you seen Tom today?'

The flock shook their heads and Baa'd in unison that they hadn't seen Tom. Oli and Tiggy continued until they reached the wall at the edge of the field.

'On you go Tiggy, you're a cat, this will be no problem for you to get over. Wait on the other side till I join you. Off you go!'

Tiggy looked at the wall then leaped up onto the top, she then looked back at Oli who nodded her head for Tiggy to go on. Tiggy jumped, twisting in the air to miss a cow pat she hadn't noticed. Landing at the side of the smelly pat she held her breath, then walked away from the disgusting smell. She found a clean place to sit, then sat and looked back at the wall. As she watched Oli's head and front legs appeared on top of the wall. Tiggy stood up and watched in amazement as Oli managed to climb and scramble over the wall. Oli fell from the top of the wall and rolled a few times then came to a stop. Tiggy rushed over to her as she was rising to her feet and laughed.

'WOOHOO. that was fun. It's been a long time since I broke out of a field, but I can still do it. This'll get Tom's attention, come on we'll soon be there.'

Tiggy shook her head and laughed, she was starting to enjoy her adventure and the company of her new friend. They headed off across the field to an open gate. As they neared the gate a farm and farm buildings came into view. Oli nodded, 'That's where we'll find Tom and some food for you.'

Chapter 4

Oli led Tiggy into the farmyard, then slowly looked around the first barn which had its doors open. Inside clucking chickens were wandering, scratching the ground, while others were jumping up and down onto hay bales. At the far end was a large pen with some calves in it. 'Wait here while I check inside,' Oli instructed as she walked into the barn. Tiggy sat down and watched Oli head towards the bottom end of the barn. Oli was looking from side to side searching for Tom.

'WHO ARE YOU?' asked a voice behind Tiggy. 'WHAT are you doing on my farm?' Tiggy slowly stood and turned to face the voice. There, sitting looking at her was a black and white collie.

Tiggy's fur rose on the back of her neck, dogs like to chase cats and Tiggy was cornered. She slowly unsheathed her claws ready to scratch the dog if it attacked.

'WELL! I asked you what you are doing in my farm. You know the humans have a saying, 'Has the cat got your tongue?' Well! you're a cat! Where's your tongue?'

Tiggy was about to reply when a voice behind her said, 'Hi, Tom, I see you've met my friend Tiggy. She's lost and needs our help to get home. Can you help? She also needs to be fed. Will you help her?'

Tom thought long and hard, stared at Oli, and then replied, 'Oli, you're a nightmare. You keep breaking out of the field and now you've brought a cat to the farm. Don't you think I've got enough to do?'

'Tom, if you help Tiggy, I promise not to escape from the field at least for a while. Honest!' Oli replied hanging her head as if she were sorry.

'Tom let out a throaty growl and replied, 'OK, but you stay in the field, no more climbing or escaping, PROMISE!'

'Okay,' Oli replied, 'I promise, as long as you help Tiggy.'

TOM

Tom growled a laugh. 'I'll help Tiggy, so you get back to the field. Off you go and no messing around, straight back.'

Oli turned to Tiggy, 'You'll be okay with Tom, he tries to be tough and grumpy, but he is really a big softy, he'll help you get safely home.'

'Get out of here!' Tom growled, 'I've got to feed Tiggy then plan her route home.'

Oli grinned at Tiggy said, 'Baaaye, and good luck.' Then she trotted out of the farmyard, a big white ball of wool heading down the track, back to her field.

'Straight to the field!' Tom shouted after her.

'Right,' Tom growled. 'Let's get you fed Tiggy then we can plan the next step in getting you home.' Tom headed off to the back of the farmhouse with Tiggy following. Around the back was Tom's kennel which had bowls of dog food, biscuits, and water. Tom sat at the kennel's entrance and nodded for Tiggy to go and eat some food. Tiggy had never eaten dog food or biscuits before, but she found them very tasty.

After being fed and a good night's sleep in the barn Tiggy woke up to the noise of the farm. She could hear a tractor in the distance, a cockerel crowing in the yard and pigeons cooing in the rafters of the barn. She stretched out, unsheathed

her claws, rolled onto her back, and yawned.

'Glad to see you're awake. I hope you had a good night's sleep, come on there's some breakfast for you.' Tom grinned and walked away.

Tiggy stood up, had one last stretch then followed Tom out of the barn. As before there was fresh food in Tom's kennel and Tom gestured for Tiggy to help herself. While Tiggy ate, Tom was looking towards the hills and sniffing the air. 'It looks like we'll get a good day to go over the hills.' Tom observed, 'When you've finished your breakfast and had a drink we'll get started. We have a long climb and a long way to go. You're sure your home is in that direction?' Tom pointed with his nose.

Tiggy sat back licked her lips looked at the sun and in the direction Tom gestured and simply said 'Yes.'

'In that case, if you're ready, let's go.' And with that Tom turned and started walking closely followed by Tiggy.

Chapter 5

They left the farmyard and headed down a track and off to the hills. As they walked Tom asked Tiggy about her home and what it was like living in a town. Tiggy described the noise and people going about their daily business and how she trained humans to feed and look after her. Tom chuckled and shook his head.

'Look around here, it's beautiful, smell the air, we can go wherever we want and meet our friends. If I had to make a choice, this is where I would stay.'

Tiggy had been looking around as Tom spoke and she liked what she saw. However, she told Tom that while everything around was beautiful, she was a Town cat.

After a while the track ended at a gate into a field, Tom walked up to the gate and stuck his head through the bars and looked around. Tiggy watched Tom as he turned and looked at her. 'Tom, what is it? I can tell by the look on your face something is wrong.

Tom gestured Tiggy to come to the gate. Tiggy looked through the gate into the field. There in the far corner was one of the biggest creatures Tiggy had ever seen. A giant of a bull with a big brass ring through his nose munching the grass. 'Who's that?' Tiggy asked

'Mad Bruce,' Tom replied in a hushed voice.

'Why do you call him Mad Bruce?' Tiggy asked still looking at Bruce. 'He looks as though he is enjoying munching the grass and he is quite relaxed.'

'That's why he's called Mad Bruce, one minute he is quiet and placid, then suddenly, with no apparent reason, he runs around headbutting everything and anyone in sight. We need to cross this field, so, let's walk very slowly and if I shout RUN! Run as fast as you can, don't look back, and get over the wall at the far side of the field.'

Tom quietly said,' Ok are you ready?' Tiggy

took a big gulp and nodded her head.

Tiggy took a last look at Mad Bruce and felt butterflies in her stomach. He was huge and she could see the powerful muscles rippling down his shoulders and body, she really didn't want to be faced by one of his charges. She followed Tom by slowly crawling under the gate into the field. The pair walked briskly across the field not speaking or looking around.

They were almost halfway across when Tom shouted, 'RUN!' The ground around them trembled as if giant hammers were hitting it. Every time Bruce's powerful hooves hit the ground his whole weight landed, sending out giant tremors, and kicking up clods of earth. Tiggy and Tom ran as fast as their four legs could carry them. The wall was getting nearer but so was Mad Bruce. They could hear him snorting and bellowing behind them and getting even closer.

At last they reached the wall. Tiggy and Tom leapt over the wall together and landed on the other side. Behind them, there was a clap like thunder and the giant stones at the top of the wall tumbled in their direction rolling across the ground. They both jumped out of the way of the stones and looked back at the wall. There was another rumble and vibration from the wall, Mad Bruce was butting the wall with his head.

Tom shouted to Tiggy, 'Come on run, the crazy bull is trying to break down the wall. Let's get out of here.' They ran across the field, leapt over a small stream then jumped over another wall into another field. They stopped and looked back. In the distance, they could see Mad Bruce had knocked a big hole in the wall and had climbed into the field behind them. He had stopped chasing them and was grazing peacefully at the side of the stream as if nothing had happened. Tom just shook his head. He was right in his description of MAD BRUCE!

Chapter 6

The pair rested for a few minutes to get their breath back then started the climb up the hill, after two hours of climbing they reached the top. Below them and as far as they could see was rolling countryside. 'See that farm in the distance,' Tom gestured with his nose 'that's where we're headed. There's someone there who'll take you on the final stretch home. And see that haze of light in the distance over the hills, it's caused by humans, that's where your home is.'

Tiggy peered into the distance, she could see the farmhouse, but the haze in the distance worried her, all the air around was so clear. Why was there a haze? They sat for a few minutes taking in the view and catching their breath after the climb. The breeze gently rippled the fur across their bodies. As she sat Tiggy reflected on her journey so far. She was surprised at how many different creatures had gone out of their way to help her. Perhaps it was a country thing. All she knew was in the town everything was noisy. She sniffed the air, it seemed so pure and fresh.

Tom had been quietly watching her. 'We are going to make a country cat out of you. You look happy and not the least bit worried that you aren't home.'

Tom's words took Tiggy by surprise. He had expressed everything Tiggy was thinking. Perhaps living in the country might not be too bad.

'Come on,' Tom said, 'We'll be there in about two hours, and we'll get something to eat and drink.' With that, Tom headed off followed closely by Tiggy.

As they walked towards the farm Tiggy found out from Tom that his hobby was competing in sheepdog trials. He explained how working with the shepherd you had to round up a small flock of sheep, guide them around various obstacles then back to the shepherd then, working with the shepherd, steer them into a pen. Tiggy was intrigued, 'And what happens if the sheep don't want to be disturbed and guided around the

SWIFT

obstacles?' she asked.

Tom chuckled, 'That's when the fun starts. You've got to get close and let them know who's the boss. Once they realise that I'm not going away and that I AM going to move them, generally, they move, and in the direction I want. The trick is to focus on one sheep, once it moves the rest follow. It is all about the fun and making sure the sheep don't get hurt. Sometimes the sheep are in the mood to play and run extremely fast, just to make me run and keep up. It's just a fun day out for everyone. Here we are, wait here, and I'll see where everyone is.'

Tom walked into the farmyard, stood, and barked several times. Suddenly round the corner of the farmhouse, skidded another collie with its tail in the air, its legs furiously scrambling to get a grip on the muddy ground as it headed to Tom. When it reached Tom both dogs jumped up balancing on their hind legs and started boxing playfully with their front legs. Tiggy was amazed, as they both settled back on their legs and rubbed their muzzles and sides together. Obviously, they knew each other. When things calmed down Tom brought the other dog over to Tiggy.

'Tiggy, this is my sister Penny. Penny this is my new friend Tiggy, I'm helping her get home. Tiggy has a general idea of where her home is, but she is a town cat and not used to the country. So, working with other animals we have formed a chain taking her in the direction of her home. Can you help us and take Tiggy on the next stage of her journey?'

'Tom, you know you don't need to ask,' Penny replied, 'if Tiggy is your friend she's my friend too. Come on let's get some food, you and Tiggy must be hungry and thirsty after your long walk over the hills.' With that Penny turned and led the trio around the farmhouse to her kennel for food and water.

Chapter 7

Tiggy looked around, it seemed as if all farms were the same, lots of sheds for the farm machinery, stalls to keep cattle in, and the farmhouse. In the farmyard, chickens were scratching on the ground. Penny's kennel was around the back of the house. Tiggy stopped, amazed, and surprised. This was no ordinary kennel. It was a small wooden shed built like a house, complete with windows and a fake chimney. Inside were cushions and blankets. Outside there were bowls of food, biscuits and water, Penny nodded to the food and said, 'Help yourself, you must be hungry after your journey.' Penny laid down with her head resting on her front paws as she watched Tom and Tiggy wolf down the food.

After five minutes of eating and drinking, Tom sat back and licked his lips while Tiggy licked her front paws and then washed her face. When Tiggy finished, she looked from Tom to Penny, 'You know if someone had said to me a few days ago, that me, a cat, would be sharing food with dogs, I would have laughed at such a stupid idea. I was brought up to run from, or fight with dogs, I don't know why but that's the way it was. The past few days have shown me that we can all get on and support each other. My journey has been such an adventure but also a revelation of how different animals can support each other. I can't thank you enough.'

Tom cleared his throat. 'Tiggy, you don't have to thank us. Living in the country we all support each other and help when we can. So, no thanks are required. Anyway, I better head back, the farmer will be back from the market and wondering where I am. Penny, I'll see you at the next sheepdog trials and perhaps Tiggy may come back and see us. Bye.' With that, Tom turned, swished his tail and headed off.

Tom's departure was so quick it took Tiggy by surprise, she looked at Penny then at the departing Tom, and she ran down the farmyard after Tom. At the entrance, she shouted, 'Tom. Thank you and

watch out for Mad Bruce on your way home.' Tom stopped, turned, grinned, waved a paw then headed for his home.

Back in the farmyard, when Tiggy reappeared Penny stood up, 'Come on Tiggy you can sleep in my kennel. There's room for two, plus it's warm and comfortable. We can continue with your journey tomorrow.' The pair headed off to Penny's kennel where both slept soundly.

The next morning Tiggy woke up and looked around, she was on her own, and there was no sign of Penny. After cleaning herself she stuck her head out of the kennel and looked around. She saw the chickens and wandered over to them, 'Have you seen Penny?' she asked the chickens. Before they could reply, a cockerel came strutting over. He had his head held high, looking at Tiggy with beady eyes.

'WHAT'S going on here? Penny woke me up this morning, ME! I'm the one that's supposed to get everyone up, that's my job. She passed me at first light before I could clear my throat to wake everyone up. So, you tell me what's going on!'

Tiggy fought back her laughter, a cockerel demanding she tells him what was going on! In the town, the cockerel would have run away from her. She was about to speak when she heard the clip, clop of horse hooves across the farmyard. Tiggy,

the cockerel and the chickens looked up, there was
Penny walking along the yard with a pony. As they
got close, the cockerel flared out the red comb
on his head, scratched the ground with his feet,
turned and huffily strutted off, head held high.

Chapter 8

The pony and Penny stopped when they reached Tiggy. 'Hi Tiggy, I've brought a friend to meet you, and to help us climb over the hills. This is Jake, he's a fell pony and he's a fantastic climber.' Tiggy looked up at Jake. The first thing she noticed was his long black mane that hung down his neck and forehead, his jet-black body glistened in the morning sun and Tiggy thought he had lovely brown eyes with long eyelashes.

'Hello Jake, I'm pleased to meet you, have you and Penny been friends for long?

'Too long to remember,' Jake replied 'But I don't see too much of her as I like to live outside on the hills. Apart from rounding up sheep Penny usually hangs around the farm. Anyway, she brought me off the hills to help you get home. She said she thinks your home is over our hills, in that direction.' Jake nodded his head.

Tiggy looked in the direction Jake had nodded and replied 'Yes, can you help me?'

'If it's over the hills no problem but I'm not going into a town. I don't like towns. They're too noisy and busy for me, but I'll get you to where you can see the town. Let's have some breakfast then get on our way.' With that Jake headed to the barn where he had oats and Penny and Tiggy shared the breakfast the farmer had put out for Penny.

After breakfast, they met in the farmyard. Jake said, 'Right Tiggy jump up on that wall.'

Tiggy looked at Penny who just nodded to the wall for Tiggy to jump on. Tiggy thought it was strange but jumped up onto the wall anyway. When she was on the wall Jake walked over and stood beside the wall. 'Now' Jake said, 'Climb onto my back and hold my mane.'

Tiggy laughed as she walked onto Jake and held his mane with her claws. 'You know I could have jumped onto your back from the ground, without climbing on the wall,' Tiggy laughed.

Jake snorted, 'Sure. But you would have used

your claws to pull yourself up, and I wouldn't like it, any way you're up now so let's go.'

And with that Jake walked out of the farmyard with Tiggy on his back holding onto his mane and Penny walking alongside.

When they cleared the farmyard Tiggy shouted, 'GIDDY UP! LET'S GO!'

Jake stopped suddenly. There was silence for a few moments then Jake slowly turned his head and focused an unblinking brown eye on Tiggy, 'Any more of that nonsense and I'll toss you off my back and you can walk. Do you understand?'

Tiggy was stunned, she hadn't meant to offend Jake, she was only joking. She mumbled in a quiet voice, 'Jake, I'm sorry I didn't mean to offend you.'

Jake burst out laughing. He nudged Tiggy with his snout, 'I was only winding you up, come on let's go!' And with that, they headed off up the hill.

Tiggy took a firm grasp of Jake's mane with her front claws and straddled his back, it was lovely and warm like riding on a magic carpet. She settled into the rhythm of his gentle walk and looked around. As they slowly climbed the hill Tiggy listened to the friendly banter between Penny and Jake. Halfway up they came across a stream, Jake stopped and looked down at the gently running

water, then gave Penny a knowing look. Penny looked up at Tiggy and nodded her head.

All the time Tiggy was watching. 'Ok, what are you two up to? You're giving each other knowing looks, and I'm sure it's something to do with me. If you're thinking of ditching me in the water, forget it. I hate water, it messes up my fur, yuk!'

Jake laughed, 'We were just thinking it would be fun to leap over the stream. However, if we get it wrong, we could end up in the water. Do you want to try real horse riding, or do you want to get off and make your own way across and watch the fun?'

'No way am I getting off, let's have some fun!'

Chapter 9

Jake and Penny turned walked back down the hill then turned again and faced back up the hill. 'Right Tiggy, get a good grip of my mane we're going to jump!'

Tiggy tightened her grip as Jake instructed then waited. Penny looked up at Jake who nodded, and then Penny exclaimed, 'Three, two, one, go!'

At that Jake and Penny ran as fast as they could towards the stream. Suddenly Tiggy felt a bit afraid. She didn't realise how fast Jake could run. She held onto his mane as tight as she could, but she was still getting bounced around on his back. Tiggy fought the temptation to dig her claws into his back as she knew it would hurt. As they ran the

noise reminded her of being chased by Mad Bruce, the sound of thunder, as Jake's hooves pounded the ground. Tiggy had a quick look down and saw Penny running alongside with a grin. Suddenly Jake leapt and there was silence, Tiggy looked down to see the glistening water flowing beneath them. They were flying. She got a glimpse of Penny alongside then all too soon they landed with a jolt on the other side. Jake slowed down and stopped. Tiggy let go of his mane and looked around. The stream was behind them and Penny alongside.

When Penny let out, 'Wha! Hoo! That was good! Jake we should do the same when we come back down!'

Tiggy joined in the laughter, it had been a bit scary, but it had been fun.

They continued until they reached the top of the hill. There before them was the town. Tiggy jumped down from Jake and sat looking at the town. 'Well, Tiggy, this is when we say goodbye, there's your town and your home, you just need to go down and you'll be safely back where you belong. Come on give Jake and I a high five then get going.'

Tiggy looked from Penny to Jake then went over and gave Penny a big cat friendly nuzzle rub and gestured for Jake to bend his head and did the same to him. 'I can't thank you and all the creatures that have helped me get here enough. Will you pass

on my thanks?'

Penny and Jake nodded yes, gave a paw, and hoof high fives, nodded then slowly turned and walked away.

From the top of the hill, Tiggy stood looking at the town through a faint haze. She could see and hear the traffic with the occasional horn tooting. She watched purposeful people walking, going to school, to the shops, and working. She also caught sight of a train slowly going into the station. Yes, this was her town and her home. She recognised the landmarks. She sat and took it all in, her home at last.

Suddenly Tiggy ran back down the hill, she ran as fast as she could without tripping or falling over. She was excited. 'WAIT FOR ME!' she shouted, 'WAIT FOR ME!'

Further down the hill Penny and Jake turned to see Tiggy running and jumping towards them, tail up in the air. They stopped and waited, something must be wrong. They thought perhaps it was the wrong town.

A breathless Tiggy caught up with them and between gulps for air said, 'I'm coming back with you, I've realised that friends are more important than living a comfortable life in town. Come on! I'm looking forward to flying over the stream again.'

With that, three different creatures, from diverse backgrounds, who had become friends, headed off, exchanging banter as they walked back down the hill and away from the town.

Geoff Swift

Geoff is the author of many 5 Star illustrated children books including: 'The Zak and Rory' series of books. Zak (a Giant Whale) and Rory (The Loch Ness Monster) meet and decide to travel the World's oceans together. They have many adventures, survive natural disasters and make new friends. Also, 'The Witch, The Cat and Jack,' a Trilogy of witch stories. An entertaining illustrated book for reading and colouring. For the younger reader, an illustrated nature and environmental series - 'Brian the Beetroot's Haircut,' 'Max the Rabbit's Close Encounters' and 'Tommy the Fieldmouse's Night-time Adventures.'

Geoff also enjoys giving school talks. Scholastic US have taken the ebook rights until 2026 of his first book 'The Friendly Giant called Zak and his Friend Rory the Misnamed Monster'. Geoff has also supported Hamleys World Book Day by giving instore author talks.

He enjoys working with Jane Cornwell the Scottish artist and illustrator.

You can follow Geoff' on Twitter: @swift_geoff

And find links to Geoff's books:
www.geoffswiftwriter.com

More books by Geoff Swift

The Zak And Rory Series

The Friendly Giant Called Zak And His Friend Rory The Misnamed Monster

Rory Never Learns

Zak And Rory's Toughest Journey

Pirates, Predators And Penguins

The Witch, The Cat And Jack

Brian The Beetroot's Haircut

Max The Rabbit's Close Encounters

Tommy The Fieldmouse's Night Time Adventures